Paganism for Beginners

The Magic Guide to the Pagan Holidays, Rituals and Spells

Table of Contents

Chapter 1: Getting to Know Paganism 6

Pagan Religion Overview..7

Wicca...7
Thelema 7
Senistrognata 8
Religious Witchcraft 8
Roman Reconstructionism (Religio Romana)........9
Kemetic or Egyptian Reconstructionism Paganism (Kemeticism) 9
Hellenic or Greek Reconstructionist Paganism (Hellenismos) 10
Gwyddons 10
Feri 11
Druidry 11
Discordianism..12
Church of All Worlds (CAW) 12
Asatru or Norse Reconstructionist Paganism......13
Other Pagan Religions 13

Typical Questions on Paganism...............................14

Where Do I Begin? 14
Is There A Difference Between Witch, Wiccan, And Pagan? 15
Do All Pagans Follow The Rede? 15
What Are Your Beliefs Concerning God and Goddesses? 16

Chapter 2: The Wheel of the Year 17

Samhain 17
Yule 18
Candlemas... 20
Ostara or Lady Day 21
Beltane or May Day.. 21
Midsummer.. 22
Mabon or Harvest Home.. 23

Chapter 3: Pagan Rituals & Spellwork 24

The Handfast Ritual... 24
Candle Magic... 27
Spells for the Practicing Witch 32

Protection Spell: Reflect Away the Harm Intended upon You 32
Weight Loss Spell: Prevent Cravings 34
Winning the Lottery: Scratch Type Magick 36

Chapter 1: Getting to Know Paganism

I am sure the question "what is paganism" is running around your mind right now. So, let me set things straight. First, paganism is not synonymous with the Wiccan. Paganism per se is not a religion, just like Christianity is not a religion. To better understand what I am saying, Christianity is use to refer to various religions that believe in Jesus Christ, examples would be the Roman Catholic religion. So, you see Christianity itself is not a religion but refers to a wide variety of religion that is based on the beliefs of Jesus Christ. This is likewise true for paganism—it is a broad term used to identify a variety of pagan religions and one of them is Wiccan, which is a widely known pagan religion.

Now, let's move on to the definition of Paganism, according to a common dictionary definition, paganism is a religion that is not Islamic, Christian, or Jewish—which is definitely true. Many people also relate paganism as earth-centered or earth-based; this is true for some pagan religion like Wicca, while for some it's not—so, it is seen as a narrow definition of paganism. According to a self-confessed pagan, the best way to describe paganism is "A pagan religion is a religion that is not Islamic, Christian, or Jewish, and self-identifies as Pagan.

Pagan Religion Overview

To help you better understand or choose which pagan religion you want to embark on, here is a list of the various pagan religions out there:

Wicca

Wicca is a contemporary Pagan religion spearheaded by Gerald Gardner in 1954. It is a pagan religion with no central authority, but coven s can have a high priest or priestess that serves as the head of each coven. Their beliefs are mainly governed by the rede, which believes in "harm none." Wiccans can practice magick or witchcraft, but it is not mandatory. Some Wicca sects believe in a god and goddess, while other sects believes and various deities.

Thelema

Thelema is another pagan religion that is based on a philosophical law known as Thelema which states that "Do what thou wilt shall be the whole of the Law. Love is the law, love under will." The law of Thelema was created by Aleister Crowley in the 1900s, wherein he believes that he is a new age prophet. Through him, he was contacted by Aiwass, a praeterhuman being and dictated a text known as "The Book of the Law."

Followers of the religion Thelema, refer to themselves as Thelemite. In Thelema, they believe in three main deities known as Ra-Hoor-Khuit, Hadit, and Nuit which is described by Crowley as a "literary convenience."

Senistrognata

Senistrognata literally means in Celtic "ancestral customs." Senistrognata is a sub-tradition of a larger religion known as the Celtic Reconstructionist Paganism. This pagan religion was brought to life by IMBAS in 2000, which is a Celtic Reconstructionist organization based in Seattle. The word imbas is an old Irish term that means "poetic inspiration." Senistrognata promotes the spiritual path of the ancestral customs of the Celtic people and it is a religious path open to agnostics, Christians, and Pagans alike.

Religious Witchcraft

Religious witchcraft is a broad term that encompasses several groups, wherein one of them is Wicca. Basically, religious witchcraft revolves around several beliefs and customs like: shared practice rather than shared belief, recognition of cycles (like cycles based on honor or core myths, self-transformation, or seasons to name a few), interaction with deities in some form, and the use of folk magic or witchcraft usually using a European context.

Roman Reconstructionism (Religio Romana)

This is a modern Pagan religious movement that bases its cult practices and worship on the pre-Christian and polytheistic religion found in Rome and its neighboring tribes and cities. Just like with any reconstructed religion, the followers of Religio refers its beliefs and customs on primary sources like Ovid, archaeological and historical evidences, with an added concession of modern sensibilities.

Kemetic or Egyptian Reconstructionism Paganism (Kemeticism)

This is basically the reconstruction of Ancient Egypt's religion which includes the revival of arts, literature, spirituality, belief systems and other relevant aspects. It is a religion based on the belief in Goddesses and Gods—the Neteru. It is also a way of living that upholds ma'at—a balance of the human society and that of the natural world and cosmos. It makes use of scholarly ways to recreate the practices and structures of the ancient religion and apply those within the contemporary era.

Hellenic or Greek Reconstructionist Paganism (Hellenismos)

This is one of the Neo-Pagan religions that center its cult practices and worship on Ancient Greece's polytheistic and traditional religion. Although the religion accepts personal intuition when it comes to spirituality, but the principal source of information comes from the works of ancient writers Hesiod, Homer, and the likes. The ritual practices of this religion are based on modern research on this religion as well as those taken from the aforementioned authors.

Gwyddons

The Gwyddon religion is more of a worship base movement rather than magic. To the Gwyddons, magic is just secondary and their primary goal is to understand what he or she is and what deity is. As a seeker, or a person who is new to the religion, will notice that the religion does not have pages of instruction nor volumes of spellwork. The student studies at his or her own pace, and a teacher is only there to help with lessons. Thus, it always falls on a student the choice and responsibility to fail or succeed. Further, the Gwyddon teachings are exact and strict. And lastly, although the student's path is sacred, this does not give him or her permission to change the Gwyddoniad teachings to suit him or her.

Feri

Feri can also be spelled as Fairy, Faerie, and Faery only strengthens the proof of the diversity of this tradition. Feri is a modern form of American Traditional Witchcraft taken from the teachings of Cora and Victor Anderson who passed on their teachings to various initiates. This religion seeks to change a person via different practices of energy work, meditation, and ritual magic through a diverse and rich spiritual art. The religion draws power from different cultures and their corresponding magical systems like Greek gnosis, Yezidi Mythology, Christian Mysticism, Celtic Folklore, Tantra, Voodoo, Conjure, Huna, and others. The adherents of this religion are initiated ritually into its mysteries.

Druidry

It is a pagan religion that seeks a spiritual practice and way that epitomizes the three greatest yearnings, namely: gain access to a source of profound wisdom, to commune deeply with the world of Nature, and to be fully creative in their lives. Each of these yearnings arrives from varying facets of yourself that you can personify as the Sage, the Shaman, and the Singer. In Druidry the Druid teachings aid in developing inner wisdom, the sage who lives within each of us; Ovate teachings aid in nurturing the shaman—the lover of nature and the healer within you; while Bardic teachings aid in developing the storyteller, the artist, or the singer within us, the creative self.

Discordianism

This is a pagan religion based on the veneration of the Goddess of Chaos—Eris Discordia and all the ideals and archetypes linked to her. Discordianism was established after the publishing of the book written by Gregory Hill, along with Kerry Wendell Thornley on 1963. The two wrote the book under the penname of Omar Khayyam Ravenhurst and Malaclypse the Younger. The religion is based on the concept of both disorder and order as illusions imposed by the human nervous system on the universe and that none of these illusions of apparent disorder and order is any more objectively true or accurate than the other.

Church of All Worlds (CAW)

In the United States the Church of All Worlds is one of the oldest incorporated Neo-Pagan religions. Their mission is to grow a network of experience, mythology, and information that gives a stimulus and context for reawakening Gaia and bringing together her children through tribal community dedicated to the evolution of consciousness and responsible stewardship.

Asatru or Norse Reconstructionist Paganism

This religion is the modern reconfiguration of the pre-Christian Germanic people's religion. The religion honors various goddesses and gods as well as helpful beings and spirits. According to the religion's beliefs there are 9 worlds which includes Asgard, the world of gods, and the Midgard, the world of the humans. What binds together all nine worlds is the World Tree. Further, there are various afterlife choices which depends upon the gods you followed while living along with other factors such as how you died and what type of person you were to name a few.

Other Pagan Religions

As I have mentioned above, the pagan religions are quite varied and numerous and here's the rest of the list: Voudon, Satanism, Santeria, Demonolatry, and Condomble.

Typical Questions on Paganism

If you have just recently discovered paganism and want to explore it, but have become stuck on where to begin (especially after reading what I have written above), then here are several common questions that people ask. The answers to these common questions will help you to identify which paganism religion best suits your needs and current beliefs.

Where Do I Begin?

This is a really common question and quite frankly has frustrated a lot of pagan newbies. But, do not worry, because I can help you figure out where to begin. Begin by introspection. Ask yourself are you interested in magical craft? Or are you looking for a religion that worships deities? Or maybe a combination of both? These are important questions that will help you decide on where to start because there are pagan religions that practice ceremonial magic or witchcraft without religious or worship overtones. There are also pagan religions that consist mostly of worshipping while there are those who combine magic or witchcraft with veneration of gods and goddesses.

Is There A Difference Between Witch, Wiccan, And Pagan?

Yes, there is. In fact, all three words mean different things. Paganism as I have mentioned earlier is not a religion, but an umbrella term used to refer to various pagan religions like Wicca. Another type of pagan religion is the Reconstructionist religions like the Kemeticism, Asatru, and Hellenismos to name a few. These Reconstructionist pagan religions are quite different from Wicca, based on their religious practices. As a matter of fact, Wicca is a religious witchcraft practice. But, you have to take note that to be Wicca does not mean you have to be a witch, neither does a witch need to be Wiccan—these two are separate entities. Witchcraft—where practitioners are called a witch, can be readily practiced together with any compatible religion or as a practice unto itself.

Do All Pagans Follow The Rede?

No. It is only the Wiccans who follow the rede of "harm none." Other pagan religions have their own system of ethics and many of them are antithetical to the rede.

What Are Your Beliefs Concerning God and Goddesses?

This is another important question you need to ponder on when looking for a pagan religion to join because each religion has various beliefs especially when it comes to gods and goddesses. There are those who believe that each god is a distinct and separate entity, some believe that all gods are really one, while there are those who believe that gods have many facets. There are also those who believe in henotheism, where you worship and believe in a single god while readily accepting the possible existence or existence of other deities that may also be served; or pantheism, where followers do not believe in a distinct anthropomorphic or personal god, but that the Universe is identical with divinity; and monotheism, where followers only believe in one god.

Chapter 2: The Wheel of the Year

The wheel of the year is generally known the pagan calendar. It consists of eight major holidays in the general Pagan calendar. So, let's take a look at each of these Sabats, or pagan holidays.

Samhain

This is the most magical night of the pagan year, which is found on the exact opposite of the Beltane (another pagan holiday) in the wheel of the year—which makes Samhain the dark twin of Beltane. Samhain is also known in many names like Halloween, Hallow E'en, All Hallow's Eve, and all hallows. During this night, it is believed as the Spirit night wherein the veil that separates the Otherworld and the human world is at its thinnest—and this makes it a night of power for those practicing witchcraft.

Samhain is a Celtic word that means 'summer's end.' But, what makes Samhain more spine-tingling is the fact that all over the world, many cultures celebrate this festival no matter what they call it. Further, this is one of those few occasions wherein the Eve of the celebration is more celebrated than the day of celebration. For example, All Hallow's Day is on Nov. 1, but Hallow's Eve is more celebrated and thus the

Halloween celebration begins at sundown of October 31. While other cultures like pre-Spanish Mexican also observe the festival of the dead on the same day. Likewise, the Egyptians also have their own celebration.

Aside from being celebrated as a sprit night, it is also celebrated as the end of the old year and the beginning of the new. As a day night of the dead, it is also believed that the dead can return to the human world if they so wish. That's why in many cultures they set an extra seat on their table for departed loved ones who may wish to visit them.

The jack-o-lantern has long been used to celebrate Halloween; its first use can be traced back to travelers using jack-o-lanterns to scare faeries or evil spirits who might lead them astray in their journey. For witches, Halloween comprises one of the 4 Greater Sabbats or High Holidays.

Yule

Yule is also known as the Midwinter Night's Eve that also coincides with the Christmas season but the day itself is celebrated earlier than December 25. During Yule, pagans celebrate the holiday with mistletoe, Yule logs, presents, caroling, and tree decorating.

They even have a nativity set, but the three central characters are Baby Sun-God, Father Time, and Mother Nature.

The real celebration of this holiday is rooted into the Winter solstice where the nights are longer than the days. It is during this time the birth of the Sun King happens. The Great Mother Nature gives birth during the longest night of the year, which symbolizes the hope for the coming lengthening days, the Light of the World, the Sacred Fire, and the new spark of hope. This is also where Christmas—as celebrated by Christians is also rooted and where many parallelisms are seen with paganism. This is the reason why the Puritans, John Calvin, and Martin Luther refuse to acknowledge and abhor Christmas.

For modern witches and pagans, Yule is celebrated during the actual Winter Solstice which usually varies year in and year out. Commonly, winter solstice occurs on or around December 21 and is considered as a Lower Holiday or Lesser Sabat in the modern Pagan calendar. But, still it is an important holiday wherein pagan customs are heartily observed. Examples of these customs are: burning of the Yule log within the first try and letting it urn for 12 hours to bring good luck; and a girl standing under a sprig of mistletoe got more than hearty kiss; also the use of the mistletoe, ivy, and evergreen which represents everlasting life and fertility.

Candlemas

Candlemas is the Christianized name for this pagan holiday, but it used to be called as Imbolc which literally means 'in the belly;' Oimelc, which means 'milk of ewes;' and Brigit's Day in honor of Brigit, the great Irish Goddess. Brigit is also known as Bride, thus she is the goddess who bestows a special patronage on any woman about to be handfasted (married)—and thus the ritual handfasting This holiday celebrates the beginning of Spring or the light returns. Thus, Candlemas is the time for the Pagan Festival of Lights.

For Witches, Candlemas is a version of the Pagan version of Valentine's Day wherein there is an emphasis on carnal frivolity. Candlemas eve falls on February 1 and the customary pagan ritual is to place a lighted candle on each and every window of the home beginning on sundown of Candlemas even. And if you like making candles, for witches this is also a good day to make them. During this day, the usual rituals are performing rites of spiritual purification and cleansing as well as creation of Brigit's crosses out of wheat or straw and hang all over the house for protection.

Ostara or Lady Day

This is also known as the vernal equinox wherein the spring season reaches its apex and once more the length of the day and night is equal. At this point, it is a pagan belief that the god of light wins the ascendancy battle between his dark twin and heralds the coming of longer days and shorter nights. And it is at this point where the great Mother goddess, who returned to her Virgin aspect in Candlemas and conceives the sun-god (who will be born on yule). For witches, Lady Day is one of the Low Holidays or Lesser Sabats of the wheel.

Beltane or May Day

In the modern witch's calendar this is among the 4 great festivals of the year. May Day is considered as the beginning of summer and is found directly across Samhain or Halloween in the wheel calendar. The common customs practiced during this pagan holiday are: maidens bathing their faces in the dew of May morning to retain their youthful beauty, drinking, music, feasting, sword dances, morris dances, archery tournaments, processions of milk maids and chimney-sweeps, repairing boundary markers and fences, and beating he bounds or walking the circuit of one's property.

For witches, this is principally a time of un-shamed fertility and sexuality and thus phallic symbolism in traditions like riding a hobby horse and Maypole.

Midsummer

Aside from the 4 great festivals of the pagan calendar, there are also 4 lesser holidays. These 4 lesser holidays (Low Holidays or Lesser Sabats) usually coincide with 2 equinoxes and 2 solstices—all of which are referred to as the 'quarter-days' of the year. Midsummer is the summer solstice, wherein the days are longest and the night is shortest and is thus a low holiday.

A customary activity during this time is to light a bonfire at sundown which wards off evil spirits while providing light to the revelers—this activity is known as "setting the watch." People often jump through these fires as a sign of good luck. Other customs are maidens picking up St. John's wort to divine a future lover, decking the front door of the house with white lilies, orpin, St. John's wort, fennel, and birch.

Lammas or Lughnasadh

The festival of the Lammas which falls on August 1 marks the beginning of fall and the end of summer. It also heralds the first harvest. It is one of the High

Holidays of Witchcraft. Lammas means "loaf-mass" because this is commonly the day where baked bread is made from the first grains of harvest of the year. In Irish Gaelic, the holiday is a feast to commemorate the funeral games of the Irish son-god Lugh—thus the name of the celebration is Lughnasadh. A common feature of this Gaelic celebration is the Tailltean marriages wherein a man and woman can live together in the same roof—like a trial marriage—until the next Lammas (a year and a day) where they can commit to each other for good or back out of the arrangement and thus bring the Tailltean marriage to a close.

Mabon or Harvest Home

It is during Mabon where the day and the night are again equal in length, which also heralds the coming of the time when the nights grow longer than the days. It is one of the pleasant holidays celebrated in pagan religion with the concept of sacrifice. Mythically speaking, this is the time of the year when the god of light is defeated by his twin—the god of darkness. At this point, it marks the time for man to rest after hard work, wherein crops have already been gathered and winter is just a month and a half away.

Chapter 3: Pagan Rituals & Spellwork

In this chapter, you will be guided and taught on how to do various pagan rituals and witchcraft. Just follow the instructions and concentrate well.

The Handfast Ritual

This is a pagan ritual that binds a woman and her man together in marriage. This will be led by a Priestess or Priest, wherein P stands for them, B for bride and G for groom.

P:
At this time and in this place
Do we call upon the Spirits of the Land
As well as the Mighty Ones of the Skies.
We call upon the Gods of our own distant past
From lands far away.
We call upon the Gods of our spiritual brethren
Who once called this place
Their own.
Witness and rejoice with us in this moment
As love is affirmed.

P: (Groom's name) and (Bride's name) step forward.

Stand before the Gods and those who witness on Earth.

P: (Groom's name), if it is your wish to become one with this woman Will you pledge your love through all that may come As long as love shall last?

G: I so pledge

P: (Bride's name), if it is your wish to become one with this man Will you pledge your love through all that may come As long as love shall last?

B: I so pledge

P: Does any say nay?

As the Gods and the Old Ones are witness
With those of us present now,
I now proclaim you man and wife
Thus are thy hands fasted...

(Commonly a piece of cord is tied around the groom and bride's hands to signify the union, thus it is called handfasting)

The Two are now One,
This work is done
And joy is yet begun!

(There is also a portion for the rings using a wand that was left out of ours but is normally placed immediately after the vows and is as follows...)

The rings are placed upon the wand before the ritual and the wand upon the altar. (This is written for both Priest and Priestess present)

The priest picks up the wand and holds one end before him in his right hand, the priestess likewise holds the other end in her left hand.

P:
Place your right hands
Over this wand...
And your rings...
His hand over hers.
Above you are the stars
Below you are the stones
As time passes, remember...
Like a star should your love burn brightly,
Like the earth should your love be firm.
Be free in giving of affection and of warmth.
Have no fear, and let not the ways or words
Of the unenlightened give you unease.
For the Gods are with you,
Now and always!

The rings are exchanged during the vows.

Candle Magic

Candle magic is easy and can be done for many and varied reasons which you will know more later. The simplest way to perform candle magic is to begin by choosing the matching candle color with your goal. The candle should be new and never used. Do not use a candle that is too big or too decorative as it might distract your concentration. Light the candle.

Then, write on a virgin piece of paper the goal of your ritual. When we say virgin that means it is new and hasn't been used or dirtied. You can make use of a colored piece of paper that matches the color of the candle you are going to use. When writing, use a magical alphabet like malachian, enochian, Theban, or others. As you write down your goal, visualize the goal coming true like a new love, a new house, a new car, the healing of a friend or family and others. Visualize the circumstances under which your goal comes true like the specifics of your new love is he kind, handsome, dark, or whatever you may want.

Once you are done writing, in a slow and deliberate fashion fold the paper and place the end of the paper on the candle's fire. As you are doing this, concentrate more on the completion of your goal. Once this is done, let the candle burn all the way. You can leave the candle to burn out just ensure that it is safe.

So, here are the candle colors and its corresponding magical uses:

- Black – used to banish negativity or evil spirits in uncrossing rituals; attracts Saturn energy; used in rituals to induce a deep meditational state; opens up the deeper levels of the unconscious
- Grey – it neutralizes a negative influence; in magic this color often sparks confusion; a neutral color useful when thinking of complex issues during meditation.
- Green – stimulates rituals for rejuvenation, harmony, money, and good luck; promotes success, fertility, and prosperity.
- Dark green – counteracts the influences of jealousy, greed, and ambition in a ritual; it is the color of jealousy, greed, and ambition.
- Emerald Green – it attracts fertility, social delights, and love.
- Blue – confers guidance and truth; useful for rituals to obtain peace, inner light, harmony, and wisdom; primary ritual color
- Light blue – use where a situation needs to be synthesized; radiates Aquarius energy; brings tranquility and peace to the home; useful in inspirational or devotional meditations; spiritual color

- Royal blue – employed to attract Jupiter energy or whenever an influence needs to be increased; color of loyalty; promotes joviality and laughter
- Indigo – useful in rituals that demand Saturn energy; use in rituals that need a deep meditational state; stops people or situations; color of inertia
- Brown – locates objects that have been lost; increases financial success; improves powers of telepathy, study, and concentration; eliminates indecisiveness; for rituals of material increase; earthy and balanced color
- Magenta – energizes rituals where spiritual healing or high levels of power and immediate action is required; it is a combination of violet and red on a high frequency
- Purple – increases Neptune energy; great for rituals to make contact with the spiritual other world or to secure financial rewards, independence, and ambition; signifies psychic manifestations, idealism, success, and power
- Silver – attracts the influence of the Mother Goddess; helps develop psychic abilities; encourages stability and removes negativity
- Red – draws Scorpio and Aries energy; increases magnetism in rituals; symbolizes will power, courage, strength, fertility, love, passion, and health

- Pink – the color of service, honor, and femininity; brings lively and friendly conversation to the dinner table; standard color for rituals to draw affections; promotes friendship and romance
- Gold – beneficial in rituals needing solar energy or to bring about fast money or luck; attracts the powers of cosmic influence and fosters understanding
- Yellow – Used in rituals where you wish to persuade someone or gain another's confidence; used in rituals that need solar energy; brings power of imagination and concentration; symbolizes unity, creativity, and activity
- White – good for rituals involving lunar energy; it can be substituted for any color candle; it is a balance of all colors; symbolizes truth seeking, healing, clairvoyance, cleansing, and spiritual enlightenment.

If you are conducting a ritual for another person who is absent because they are located far away, you can still conduct the ritual for that person by using another candle to symbolically represent that absent person. An example of which is a healing ritual for a loved one located far away. All you have to do is make sure of the absent person's birthdate and its corresponding zodiac sign. Each zodiac sign is represented by a color as follows:

- Pisces – mauve
- Aquarius – all colors
- Capricorn – black
- Sagittarius – purple
- Scorpio – red
- Libra – pink
- Virgo – yellow
- Leo – orange
- Cancer – silver
- Gemini – yellow
- Taurus – green
- Aries – red

Spells for the Practicing Witch

Protection Spell: Reflect Away the Harm Intended upon You

Materials:
Sandalwood incense
1 black candle
2 small mirrors, ideally on stands

Incantation:
The magick upon me
Be trapped this night
Between these mirrors
Never see light

Instructions:

1) Light up the incense and let the aroma build up a bit around your altar.
2) Into the candle, carve a deep X.
3) Set up the two mirrors in a way that they face each other with the candle in between them. Repeating candles should be seen deep within the mirrors.
4) Light the candle, focus on the negative magick you are trying to reverse as you focus your gaze back and forth between the mirrors.

5) As you concentrate, chant the incantation over and over again is you visualize the curse being reflected back to the sender.
6) Let the candle burn all the way through. Leave the mirrors facing one another for a month.

Weight Loss Spell: Prevent Cravings

Do this spell during a waning moon, that's anytime within the 2-weeks after a full moon. The spell is best done outside, but near a window is also fine. This will help you curb your cravings while on a weight loss mission.

Materials:
A green bag or pouch
A green candle
A piece of clear quartz

Incantation:
Goddess within
Goddess without
Guide me to my goal
Easy my hunger
Soothe my spirit
Strengthen my resolve
As I wish it, so mote it be

Instructions:

1) While holding the crystal, light the candle and look up at the moon.
2) Repeat the incantation as you watch the moon while also concentrating on eating healthier and losing weight.

3) Further, think about the foods you crave and usually have difficulty resisting. Think of getting stronger resolve around these foods and send that energy into the crystal.
4) When you are done, turn off the candle and place the crystal in a green bag.
5) Carry that green bag with the crystal, tucked in your pocket, wherever you go.
6) If the spell is doing well, recharge the stone after a month.

Winning the Lottery: Scratch Type Magick

This is specific for the scratch type ticket, so before you go out and buy the scratch ticket, do this spell first to help guide you pick the winning scratch ticket.

Materials:
A small piece of malachite
5 dry corn kernels
3 acorns

Incantation:
Nuts and seeds
Where wealth leads,
Mix and match,
Choose a scratch

Instructions:

1) In between both your hands, hold the malachite, corn kernels, and acorns. Rub your hands together without letting them fall as you chant the incantation.
2) Continue rubbing your hands, but this time slowly let out all the acorn, corn kernels, and malachite.
3) Buy your scratch ticket the next day, but before doing so hold the malachite in your palm as you pick out the scratch ticket.

Copyright © 2015. All rights reserved.

Except as permitted under the United States Copyright Act of 1976, reproduction or utilization of this work in any form or by any electronic, mechanical, or other means, now known or hereafter invented, including xerography, photocopying, and recording, and in any information storage and retrieval system, is forbidden without written permission.

The ideas, concepts, and opinions expressed in this book are intended to be used for educational and reference purposes only. Author and publisher claim no responsibility to any person or entity for any liability, loss, or damage caused or alleged to be caused directly or indirectly as a result of the use, application, or interpretation of the material in this book.

Printed in Great Britain
by Amazon